The Complete Guide to Microsoft Office 365 for Beginners:

Enhance Your Productivity in 2023

Disclaimer Notice:

Please note the information contained within this document is for educational and entertainment purposes only. All effort has been executed to present accurate, up to date, and reliable, complete information. No warranties of any kind are declared or implied. Readers acknowledge that the author is not engaging in the rendering of legal, financial, medical or professional advice. The content within this book has been derived from various sources. Please consult a licensed professional before attempting any techniques outlined in this book.

By reading this document, the reader agrees that under no circumstances is the author responsible for any losses, direct or indirect, which are incurred as a result of the use of information contained within this document, including, but not limited to, — errors, omissions, or inaccuracies.

Table of Contents

Chapter 1 - Introduction to Microsoft Office 365

Microsoft Office 365 is a cloud-based suite of productivity tools that includes the latest versions of popular Office apps like Word, Excel, PowerPoint, and more. It is designed to help individuals, teams, and organizations work efficiently and collaborate effectively, regardless of location or device.

In this chapter, we will take a closer look at the key features of Office 365 and why it has become such a popular choice for businesses and individuals alike. We will also discuss the various Office 365 plans and options available to help you choose the best one for your needs.

Key Features of Office 365

- Access to the latest versions of Word, Excel, PowerPoint, and other popular Office apps

- 1 TB of storage per user with OneDrive for Business

- Collaboration tools like Teams, OneNote, and Planner

- Email and calendar capabilities with Outlook Online

- Mobile app versions of Office apps for iOS and Android

- Security features such as data protection and compliance tools

Benefits of Using Office 365

- Increased productivity and efficiency through the use of latest Office tools and collaboration features

- Improved collaboration and teamwork, even for remote or mobile workers

- Access to files and data from anywhere, on any device

- Peace of mind with robust security and data protection features

Office 365 Plans and Options

- Office 365 Home: designed for personal use, includes Word, Excel, PowerPoint, and more for up to 6 users

- Office 365 Business: designed for small businesses, includes Office apps and email with 50 GB of storage

- Office 365 Business Premium: includes additional security and device management features for small businesses

- Office 365 Enterprise: includes advanced security and compliance features for larger organizations

With its robust set of features and benefits, Office 365 is a powerful tool for anyone looking to improve their productivity and collaboration. In the following chapters, we will dive deeper into the individual components of Office 365, including how to get started, how to use the various Office apps, and how to get the most out of the platform.

By the end of this book, you will have a solid understanding of how to use Office 365 to enhance your productivity and improve your workflow.

Using Office 365 on Different Devices One of the key advantages of Office 365 is its compatibility with a wide range of devices. Whether you prefer to work on a laptop or desktop computer, a tablet, or a smartphone, Office 365 has you covered. You can access your files, data, and apps from anywhere, and the interface will be consistent and easy to use no matter what device you're using.

With Office 365, you can work online or offline, and your changes will be synced across all devices when you next connect. This makes it easy to pick up right where you left off, even if you're working on a different device. Additionally, the Office apps are optimized for touch-based devices, making it easy to work on-the-go.

Getting Started with Office 365 Getting started with Office 365 is straightforward and simple. Once you have an account, you can log in to the Office 365 portal from any web browser. From here, you can access all of your apps, files, and data, as well as manage your account settings.

If you're new to Office 365, we recommend taking some time to explore the user interface and get familiar with the various apps and features. You may also want to take advantage of the various tutorials and resources available through the Office 365 support center to help you get up and running quickly.

In the following chapters, we will cover each of the key components of Office 365 in detail, including how to use Word, Excel, PowerPoint, OneDrive, and more. Whether you're new to the Office suite of tools or a seasoned user, you'll find plenty of helpful tips and tricks to help you make the most of Office 365.

Office 365 is a comprehensive and powerful suite of productivity tools that can help you work more efficiently and effectively. With its cloud-based architecture and wide range of features, Office 365 is a smart choice for anyone looking to improve their workflow and collaborate more effectively with others.

In this chapter, we've taken a closer look at what Office 365 is, its key features and benefits, and the various plans and options available. Whether you're a small business owner looking to improve productivity and collaboration, or an individual looking to work more efficiently, Office 365 is a comprehensive and powerful tool that can help you achieve your goals.

In the following chapters, we'll dive into each of the individual components of Office 365 in more detail. From getting started with Office apps like Word, Excel, and PowerPoint, to using OneDrive to store and share files, to communicating and collaborating with Teams, we'll cover everything you need to know to get the most out of Office 365.

By the end of this book, you'll have a solid understanding of how to use Office 365 to enhance your productivity, streamline your workflow, and work more effectively with others. So, let's get started!

Chapter 2 - Setting Up Your Office 365 Account

Setting up your Office 365 account is the first step to getting started with this comprehensive and powerful suite of productivity tools. In this chapter, we'll walk you through the process of setting up your account, from choosing the right plan for your needs to logging in and getting started with the Office 365 portal.

Choosing the Right Plan Before setting up your Office 365 account, it's important to choose the right plan that meets your needs and budget. There are several different plans available, ranging from basic plans that include access to the essential Office apps, to premium plans that include additional features such as advanced security and admin controls.

When choosing a plan, it's important to consider the number of users you need to provide access to, as well as the type of data you'll be working with and storing. Additionally, you'll want to consider any specific needs you have, such as advanced email capabilities, audio and video conferencing, and more.

To help you choose the right plan, Microsoft provides a comprehensive comparison of the different Office 365 plans on their website. Be sure to take the time to review these options and choose the plan that best fits your needs.

Creating Your Account Once you've chosen the right plan for your needs, you can create your Office 365 account by following these simple steps:

1. Go to the Office 365 website and click on the "Sign up" button.

2. Enter your personal information, including your email address and a password.

3. Choose the plan you want to subscribe to.

4. Enter your billing information and complete the payment process.

5. Confirm your account by clicking on the link sent to your email.

Once your account is confirmed, you'll be taken to the Office 365 portal, where you can start using the various apps and features of the suite.

Getting Started with the Office 365 Portal The Office 365 portal is your starting point for accessing all of the apps and features of the suite. From the portal, you can access your email, files, and other data, as well as manage your account settings.

When you first log in to the Office 365 portal, you'll be asked to set up your profile, including your name and profile picture. You can also add or change your email signature and customize your notifications.

The Office 365 portal also provides you with quick access to all of the apps and services you have access to, including Word, Excel, PowerPoint, OneDrive, and more. Simply click on the app you want to use to open it, or use the search bar at the top of the screen to find what you're looking for.

Conclusion In this chapter, we've covered the process of setting up your Office 365 account, from choosing the right plan for your needs to getting started with the Office 365 portal. With your account set up and ready to go, you're now ready to start using the various apps and features of the suite to enhance your productivity and streamline your workflow.

In the following chapters, we'll dive into each of the individual components of Office 365 in more detail, and show you how to use these tools to work more efficiently and effectively. So, let's get started!

Chapter 3 - Getting to Know the Office 365 User Interface

The Office 365 user interface is the first thing you'll see when you log into the suite of productivity tools. In this chapter, we'll take a closer look at the Office 365 user interface, including the main elements and features, and show you how to navigate and use it effectively.

The Office 365 User Interface The Office 365 user interface is a web-based interface that provides you with access to all of the apps and features of the suite. When you log in to the Office 365 portal, you'll be taken to the user interface, which consists of the following main elements:

- App Launcher: The app launcher provides you with quick access to all of the apps and services you have access to, including Word, Excel, PowerPoint, OneDrive, and more. Simply click on the app you want to use to open it.

- Navigation Bar: The navigation bar provides you with access to various settings and options, including your profile, settings, and help. You can also use the search bar at the top of the screen to find what you're looking for.

9

- Tiles: The tiles on the Office 365 user interface provide you with information about your recent activity, as well as quick access to your files, email, and other data.

- Dashboard: The dashboard provides you with an overview of your recent activity, including new emails, file updates, and other notifications. You can also use the dashboard to quickly access your most frequently used apps and services.

Navigating the Office 365 User Interface Navigating the Office 365 user interface is simple and straightforward. To access an app or service, simply click on the app launcher and choose the app you want to use. You can also use the search bar at the top of the screen to find what you're looking for.

To access your settings and options, click on the navigation bar at the top of the screen and choose the option you want to use. For example, you can access your profile, change your email signature, and customize your notifications from the settings option.

Working with the Tiles The tiles on the Office 365 user interface provide you with quick access to your files, email, and other data. You can use the tiles to quickly find the information you need, as well as to access your recent activity.

To work with a tile, simply click on it to open the app or service it corresponds to. For example, clicking on the OneDrive tile will open your OneDrive account, where you can access and manage your files.

Conclusion In this chapter, we've covered the Office 365 user interface, including the main elements and features, and shown you how to navigate and use it effectively. By understanding the Office 365 user interface, you'll be able to work more efficiently and effectively with the suite of productivity tools.

In the following chapters, we'll dive into each of the individual components of Office 365 in more detail, and show you how to use these tools to enhance your productivity and streamline your workflow. So, let's get started!

Chapter 4 - Working with Word Online

Introduction Word Online is a powerful online version of Microsoft Word that allows you to create, edit, and share documents from anywhere, on any device. In this chapter, we'll take a closer look at Word Online and show you how to use its features to create and edit professional-looking documents.

Getting Started with Word Online To start using Word Online, simply log in to your Office 365 account and click on the Word Online app. When you open Word Online, you'll see a screen similar to this:

The Word Online interface is similar to the desktop version of Word, but with a few key differences. The most notable difference is that the ribbon at the top of the screen is simplified, with only the most commonly used commands and options.

Creating a New Document To create a new document in Word Online, click on the "Blank Document" option. You can also choose to start from a template, if you prefer.

Working with Text In Word Online, you can format and edit text in much the same way you would in the desktop version of Word. To format text, simply select the text you want to format and use the options in the ribbon at the top of the screen to apply bold, italic, underline, and other formatting options.

You can also use the Paragraph section of the ribbon to control paragraph formatting, such as indentation, spacing, and alignment.

Working with Tables Word Online also allows you to create and work with tables. To insert a table, click on the "Insert" tab in the ribbon and choose "Table." You can then choose the number of rows and columns you want in your table and add text, data, or other content.

You can format tables in Word Online just as you would in the desktop version of Word. For example, you can change the color and borders of cells, as well as adjust the size and orientation of columns and rows.

Working with Images Word Online also allows you to insert and work with images. To insert an image, click on the "Insert" tab in the ribbon and choose "Picture." You can then select the image you want to insert from your computer or OneDrive.

Once an image is inserted, you can use the options in the ribbon to adjust its size, position, and formatting. You can also use the Picture Tools tab to add effects, borders, and other enhancements to your images.

Saving and Sharing Documents When you're done working on a document, you can save it to your OneDrive or another cloud-based storage service, or download it to your computer. To save your document, click on the "File" tab in the ribbon and choose "Save."

Collaborating with Others One of the great benefits of using Word Online is the ability to collaborate with others in real-time. This means that multiple people can work on the same document at the same time, making it easier to work together on projects and assignments.

To collaborate with others in Word Online, simply share your document with them and give them permission to edit it. You can see who is currently working on the document by checking the "Collaborators" section in the "Share" pane.

In Word Online, you can also use the "Comments" feature to provide feedback and make suggestions on a document. To add a comment, simply highlight the text you want to comment on and click on the "Insert Comment" button in the "Review" tab. You can then type your comment and reply to comments made by others.

Working with Styles Styles are a powerful feature in Word Online that allow you to quickly and easily apply consistent formatting to your documents. To use styles, simply click on the "Home" tab in the ribbon and choose a style from the "Styles" section.

For example, you can use the "Heading 1" style to format the main headings in your document, and the "Normal" style for your body text. By using styles, you can ensure that your document has a consistent look and feel, even if you make changes to the formatting later.

Using Templates Another way to make the most of Word Online is to use templates. Templates are pre-made documents that you can use as a starting point for your own documents. To use a template, simply click on the "File" tab in the ribbon and choose "New" to see a list of available templates.

For example, you can use a template to create a resume, business letter, or report. Templates are a great way to save time and get professional results, and they can be customized to meet your specific needs.

Working with Footnotes and Endnotes Word Online also allows you to add footnotes and endnotes to your documents. Footnotes are notes that appear at the bottom of the page, while endnotes appear at the end of the document. To add a footnote or endnote, click on the "References" tab in the ribbon and choose "Insert Footnote" or "Insert Endnote."

Footnotes and endnotes can be used to provide additional information or to cite sources in your document. In Word Online, you can easily format and manage your footnotes and endnotes using the options in the "References" tab.

Conclusion In this chapter, we've covered many of the key features of Word Online, including how to create and edit documents, work with styles and templates, collaborate with others, and use footnotes and endnotes. By mastering these features, you'll be able to create professional-looking documents and work more efficiently with others.

Chapter 5 - Advanced Features in Word Online

Working with Tables Tables are a useful way to organize information in a structured format. Word Online includes many tools for working with tables, making it easy to create and edit them.

To create a table, click on the "Insert" tab in the ribbon and choose "Table." You can then select the number of rows and columns you want in your table. Once you have created your table, you can format it using the options in the "Table Tools" tab that appears when you select the table.

For example, you can change the border style and color, add shading, and format the text in your table. You can also use the "Table Layout" section in the "Table Tools" tab to adjust the width of your columns and the height of your rows.

Working with Columns In Word Online, you can also format your document into columns, just like in a newspaper. To create columns in your document, click on the "Page Layout" tab in the ribbon and choose "Columns." You can then select the number of columns you want, as well as the column width and spacing.

Working with Styles and Themes As mentioned in the previous chapter, styles are a powerful tool for formatting your documents. In addition to styles, Word Online also includes themes, which are collections of coordinated styles and colors.

To apply a theme to your document, click on the "Page Layout" tab in the ribbon and choose "Themes." You can then select the theme you want to use, and all of the styles in your document will be updated to match.

Working with SmartArt SmartArt is a tool in Word Online that allows you to create visual representations of information, such as flow charts, organization charts, and lists. To create SmartArt, click on the "Insert" tab in the ribbon and choose "SmartArt." You can then select the type of SmartArt you want to create and add your information.

SmartArt is a great way to add visual interest to your documents and make complex information easier to understand. In Word Online, you can format your SmartArt using the options in the "SmartArt Tools" tab that appears when you select the SmartArt.

Working with Charts Another way to present information in Word Online is by using charts. Charts allow you to display data in a visual format, such as bar charts, line charts, and pie charts. To create a chart, click on the "Insert" tab in the ribbon and choose "Chart." You can then select the type of chart you want to create and enter your data.

In Word Online, you can format your chart using the options in the "Chart Tools" tab that appears when you select the chart. You can change the style of your chart, add labels and data markers, and format the colors and borders.

Working with Images Images can help make your documents more visually appealing and engaging. In Word Online, you can insert images from your computer or from the web. To insert an image, click on the "Insert" tab in the ribbon and choose "Picture."

Once you have inserted an image into your document, you can format it using the options in the "Picture Tools" tab that appears when you select the image. For example, you can change the size and aspect ratio, add a border, and adjust the brightness and contrast.

Working with Shapes Shapes are another way to add visual interest to your documents. Word Online includes many different shapes, such as rectangles, circles, arrows, and stars. To insert a shape, click on the "Insert" tab in the ribbon and choose "Shapes."

Once you have inserted a shape into your document, you can format it using the options in the "Drawing Tools" tab that appears when you select the shape. For example, you can change the fill and outline colors, add a shadow, and adjust the size and rotation.

Working with Headers and Footers Headers and footers are sections of your document that appear at the top and bottom of each page. You can use headers and footers to add information such as page numbers, date and time, and document title. To add a header or footer, click on the "Insert" tab in the ribbon and choose "Header & Footer."

Once you have added a header or footer, you can type in the information you want to include. You can also format your headers and footers using the options in the "Header & Footer Tools" tab that appears when you are working in this section of your document.

Working with Page Backgrounds In Word Online, you can also change the background color or pattern of your pages. To change the page background, click on the "Page Layout" tab in the ribbon and choose "Page Color." You can then select the color or pattern you want to use.

Working with Page Borders In addition to changing the background color of your pages, you can also add a border to your pages. To add a page border, click on the "Page Layout" tab in the ribbon and choose "Page Borders." You can then select the border style, color, and width you want to use.

Conclusion In this chapter, we've covered more advanced features of Word Online, including working with images, shapes, headers and footers, page backgrounds, and page borders. With these tools at your disposal, you'll be able to create even more visually appealing and professional-looking documents in Word

Online. Whether you're creating reports, presentations, or just everyday documents, these advanced features will help you to take your Word Online skills to the next level.

Chapter 6 - Creating and Formatting Spreadsheets with Excel Online

Introduction

Excel Online is the web-based version of Microsoft's popular spreadsheet software, Excel. It provides a range of tools for creating and formatting spreadsheets, and allows you to work with your spreadsheets from anywhere with an internet connection. In this chapter, we'll cover the basics of using Excel Online, including creating and formatting spreadsheets, entering data, and using simple formulas.

Getting Started

To get started with Excel Online, you'll need to log into your Office 365 account and select the Excel Online app. When you open Excel Online, you'll see a new, blank spreadsheet.

Entering Data

Entering data into an Excel Online spreadsheet is similar to entering data into any other spreadsheet program. You can simply click on a cell and type in the data you want to enter. To move to another cell, use the arrow keys or your mouse.

Formatting Cells

Excel Online provides a range of tools for formatting your cells, including font size, font color, background color, and cell borders. To format a cell, simply select the cell or cells you want to format and use the options in the "Home" tab in the ribbon.

Creating Formulas

Formulas are the key to working with spreadsheets. With formulas, you can perform calculations and analyze your data. In Excel Online, you can use a variety of formulas, including basic arithmetic formulas, financial formulas, and statistical formulas.

To create a formula in Excel Online, start by selecting the cell where you want the formula to appear. Then, type in the formula using the appropriate syntax, such as "=A1+B1" to add the contents of cells A1 and B1. When you press "Enter," Excel Online will calculate the result of the formula and display it in the selected cell.

Saving and Sharing Spreadsheets

Once you have created and formatted your spreadsheet, you can save it to your OneDrive account or share it with others. To save your spreadsheet, click on the "File" tab in the ribbon and choose "Save." To share your spreadsheet, click on the "File" tab in the ribbon and choose "Share." From there, you can invite others to view or edit your spreadsheet by entering their email addresses.

Working with Charts Excel Online provides a range of tools for creating charts and visualizing your data. Charts can help you quickly understand your data and make informed decisions based on that data. In Excel Online, you can create a variety of charts, including bar charts, line charts, pie charts, and more.

To create a chart in Excel Online, select the data you want to use for the chart and then click on the "Insert" tab in the ribbon. From there, you can select the type of chart you want to create and customize it as needed. For example, you can change the chart's title, axis labels, and legend. You can also format the chart's appearance by changing the colors, font size, and more.

Working with Tables Tables are a great way to organize and analyze your data in Excel Online. With tables, you can sort, filter, and summarize your data, making it easier to understand and work with.

To create a table in Excel Online, select the data you want to use for the table and then click on the "Insert" tab in the ribbon. From there, you can select the "Table" option and choose the style you want for your table. Excel Online will then create a table based on your data and you can start working with it right away.

Working with PivotTables PivotTables are a powerful tool in Excel Online that allow you to analyze and summarize large amounts of data. With PivotTables, you can group your data by specific fields, calculate totals and subtotals, and create charts to visualize your data.

To create a PivotTable in Excel Online, select the data you want to use for the PivotTable and then click on the "Insert" tab in the ribbon. From there, you can select the "PivotTable" option and choose the location for your PivotTable. Excel Online will then create a PivotTable based on your data and you can start working with it right away.

PivotTables are a powerful and versatile tool in Excel that allow you to quickly summarize and analyze large amounts of data. With PivotTables, you can quickly create dynamic, interactive reports that can help you make informed decisions based on your data. In this chapter, we will cover the basics of PivotTables and how to use them in Excel Online.

Getting Started with PivotTables

To start using PivotTables, you will first need to create a new worksheet and import or enter your data into it. Your data should be organized into columns with headers, and should be formatted as a table or listed range.

Once your data is ready, you can create a PivotTable by clicking on the "Insert" tab and selecting "PivotTable" from the "Tables" section. You will then be prompted to select your data source and choose where you would like your PivotTable to be placed.

Working with the PivotTable Field List

Once you have created your PivotTable, you will see a new "PivotTable Field List" on the right side of your screen. This list contains all of the fields in your data source and allows you to add, remove, and reorganize fields as needed.

To add a field to your PivotTable, simply drag and drop the field from the field list into the "Rows" or "Columns" section. You can also add a field to the "Values" section to aggregate the data in that field. For example, you can add a "Sum of Sales" column to see the total sales for each group of data.

Filtering and Sorting PivotTable Data

PivotTables allow you to filter and sort your data to highlight specific information and help you make informed decisions. To filter your data, simply click on the drop-down arrow in the field header and select the items you would like to include or exclude. You can also sort your data by clicking on the field header and selecting "Sort A to Z" or "Sort Z to A".

Working with PivotCharts

PivotCharts are interactive charts that are linked to a PivotTable. You can use PivotCharts to visualize and analyze your data in a way that is easy to understand. To create a PivotChart, simply click on the "Insert" tab and select "PivotChart" from the "Charts" section. You will then be prompted to select your data source and choose the type of chart you would like to create.

Updating and Refreshing PivotTables

It is important to note that PivotTables are dynamic and will update automatically when you change the data in your source. However, if you make changes to your data source outside of Excel, you may need to refresh your PivotTable to see the updated data. To refresh a PivotTable, simply right-click anywhere in the PivotTable and select "Refresh".

PivotTables are a powerful and versatile tool in Excel that allow you to quickly summarize and analyze large amounts of data. Whether you are working with sales data, customer data, or any other type of data, PivotTables can help you make informed decisions and get more insights from your data. By following the steps outlined in this chapter, you should now have a good understanding of how to create and work with PivotTables in Excel Online.

Working with Formulas and Functions One of the key strengths of Excel is its ability to perform complex calculations using formulas and functions. With formulas and functions, you can perform tasks such as adding, subtracting, multiplying, and dividing numbers, as well as performing more complex calculations such as finding the average, sum, or maximum of a set of numbers.

Understanding Excel Formulas and Functions

Excel is a powerful tool for data analysis and management, and one of the key ways it accomplishes this is through the use of formulas and functions. In this chapter, we will explore what formulas and functions are, how they work, and some of the most commonly used functions in Excel.

What are Excel Formulas?

An Excel formula is a set of instructions that tells Excel how to perform a calculation. Formulas are entered into a cell and begin with an equal sign (=). For example, to add the values in cells A1 and B1, you would enter the formula =A1 + B1 into a cell. When the formula is entered, Excel will perform the calculation and display the result in the cell.

What are Excel Functions?

An Excel function is a pre-written formula that performs a specific calculation. Functions are entered into a cell in the same way as formulas, but instead of using a simple equation, you use a function name, followed by its arguments in parentheses. For example, to find the average of a range of cells, you would use the AVERAGE function, like so: =AVERAGE(A1:A10).

Commonly Used Functions in Excel

1. SUM: Adds together a range of values. For example, =SUM(A1:A10) adds together the values in cells A1 through A10.

2. AVERAGE: Calculates the average of a range of values. For example, =AVERAGE(A1:A10) calculates the average of the values in cells A1 through A10.

3. MAX: Returns the highest value in a range of values. For example, =MAX(A1:A10) returns the highest value in cells A1 through A10.

4. MIN: Returns the lowest value in a range of values. For example, =MIN(A1:A10) returns the lowest value in cells A1 through A10.

5. IF: Allows you to perform conditional calculations. For example, =IF(A1>10, "Greater than 10", "Less than 10") returns "Greater than 10" if the value in cell A1 is greater than 10, and "Less than 10" if it is not.

6. VLOOKUP: Searches for a value in the first column of a table, and returns a value from a specified column in the same row. For example, =VLOOKUP(A1, B1:D10, 2, TRUE) searches for the value in cell A1 in the first column of the table in cells B1 through D10, and returns the value in the second column of the same row.

7. INDEX/MATCH: A combination of the INDEX and MATCH functions, used to find a value in a table and return a value from a specified column in the same row.

These are just a few of the many functions available in Excel, and there are many others that can be used for specific tasks, such as financial, statistical, and date and time calculations.

Conclusion

Excel formulas and functions are a key tool for data analysis and management in Excel. Whether you are using a simple formula to perform a calculation, or a complex function to analyze data, it is important to understand how they work and how to use them effectively. With practice and a little bit of learning, you can become an Excel master, able to tackle even the most complex data challenges.

Working with Charts and Graphs Another great feature of Excel is its ability to create charts and graphs that help you visualize your data. With charts and graphs, you can quickly see patterns and trends in your data, and communicate your findings to others in a clear and concise way.

Excel is a powerful tool for data analysis, and one of its strengths is the ability to create visually appealing charts and graphs to represent your data. These charts and graphs can help you quickly identify trends and patterns in your data, and make it easier to communicate your findings to others. In this chapter, we'll explore how to create and format charts and graphs in Excel Online.

Getting Started with Charts

To create a chart in Excel Online, first, select the data you want to include in your chart. This could be a single range of cells, or multiple ranges if you want to include data from multiple sources. Once your data is selected, click on the "Insert" tab on the ribbon and select the type of chart you want to create. There are many different types of charts to choose from, including column charts, line charts, bar charts, pie charts, and more.

Formatting Charts

Once you've created your chart, you can format it to make it look exactly how you want. There are many formatting options to choose from, including changing the colors and styles of the chart elements, adding or removing data labels and gridlines, and changing the axis labels. To format your chart, simply right-click on the chart and select "Format Chart Area". From here, you can select different options to customize your chart.

Adding Data to Your Chart

You can add more data to your chart by simply selecting the new data and clicking the "Refresh Data" button on the "Data" tab on the ribbon. This will add the new data to your chart and update it to reflect any changes.

Using Sparklines

In addition to creating full-size charts, Excel Online also allows you to create small, in-cell charts called Sparklines. Sparklines are a great way to quickly show trends in your data without taking up much space. To create a Sparkline, select the data you want to include in your chart, then click on the "Insert" tab on the ribbon and select "Sparklines". You can then choose the type of Sparkline you want to create and format it just like you would a full-size chart.

Excel's Chart Tools

Excel Online also has a set of chart tools that you can use to further customize your charts and graphs. These tools allow you to add trendlines, error bars, and more to your charts, as well as customize the data labels and axis labels. To access the chart tools, simply right-click on your chart and select "Format Chart

Area". From here, you can select the "Chart Tools" tab to access these advanced features.

Excel Online's ability to create visually appealing charts and graphs is one of its strengths, and can help you quickly identify trends and patterns in your data. Whether you're creating full-size charts or in-cell Sparklines, Excel Online has the tools you need to make your data come to life. With its intuitive interface and wide range of formatting options, you'll be able to create charts and graphs that effectively communicate your findings to others.

Working with Conditional Formatting Conditional formatting is a feature in Excel that allows you to apply formatting to cells based on certain conditions. For example, you could use conditional formatting to highlight cells that contain values that are above or below a certain threshold.

To use conditional formatting in Excel Online, you first need to select the cells you want to format. Once you've selected the cells, you can then choose the "Conditional Formatting" option from the "Home" tab in the ribbon. From there, you can select the type of conditional formatting you want to use and specify the conditions that should trigger the formatting.

Conclusion

With these advanced features, you can take your Excel skills to the next level and create even more powerful and interactive spreadsheets. Whether you're working with formulas and functions, charts and graphs, or conditional formatting, Excel Online has the tools you need to get the job done. So start exploring these features today and discover all the ways you can enhance your productivity with Excel Online.

Chapter 7 - Working with PowerPoint Online

PowerPoint is a powerful presentation software that allows you to create professional-looking slideshows with ease. With PowerPoint Online, you can access the same features and functionality as the desktop version of PowerPoint, but with the added convenience of being able to work from anywhere with an internet connection.

Getting Started with PowerPoint Online To get started with PowerPoint Online, simply log in to your Office 365 account and open the PowerPoint Online app. From there, you can create a new presentation, or open an existing one.

Working with Slides In PowerPoint Online, you work with slides to create your presentation. A slide is a single page in your presentation that contains text, images, charts, and other elements. To add a new slide to your presentation, simply click the "New Slide" button in the Home tab.

Formatting Text and Shapes In PowerPoint, you can format text and shapes in a variety of ways to make your presentation look more professional. For example, you can change the font, color, and size of text, as well as add borders and background colors to shapes. To format text and shapes in PowerPoint Online, simply select the element you want to format and use the options in the Home tab.

Working with Images and Media Images and media can add a dynamic touch to your presentation and help you communicate your message more effectively. In PowerPoint Online, you can insert images, videos, and audio clips into your slides. To insert an image or media file, simply click the "Insert" tab and select the type of file you want to insert.

Adding Transitions and Animations Transitions and animations can help bring your presentation to life and make it more engaging. In PowerPoint Online, you can add a variety of transitions and animations to your slides to make them more dynamic. To add a transition or animation, simply select the slide you want to add it to and choose the "Animations" tab. From there, you can select the transition or animation you want to use.

Working with Charts and Graphs Charts and graphs can help you present data in a clear and concise way. In PowerPoint Online, you can insert a variety of charts and graphs into your slides, including bar charts, line charts, and pie charts. To insert a chart or graph, simply click the "Insert" tab and select the type of chart or graph you want to insert.

Working with Master Slides In PowerPoint Online, you can create a master slide that serves as a template for the rest of your presentation. This is useful for creating a consistent look and feel for your slides. To create a master slide, go to the "View" tab and select "Slide Master." From there, you can format the elements of your master slide, such as the background, font, and colors. Any changes you make to the master slide will automatically be applied to the rest of your slides.

Using Themes Themes are pre-designed templates that you can apply to your presentation to give it a professional look and feel. PowerPoint Online includes a variety of themes that you can use to enhance your presentation. To apply a theme, go to the "Design" tab and select "Themes." From there, you can browse through the available themes and select the one you want to use.

Adding Speaker Notes Speaker notes are a great way to keep track of your thoughts and ideas as you prepare for a presentation. In PowerPoint Online, you can add speaker notes to each slide in your presentation. To add speaker notes, simply go to the "View" tab and select "Speaker Notes." From there, you can type in your notes for each slide.

Using the Presenter View The Presenter View is a feature in PowerPoint Online that allows you to view your presentation and speaker notes on one screen, while the audience sees only the slides on another screen. To use the Presenter View, go to the "Slide Show" tab and select "Presenter View." From there, you can view your slides and speaker notes, as well as control the flow of your presentation.

Exporting and Sharing Your Presentation Once you've finished creating your presentation, you may want to share it with others or export it for use on a different device. In PowerPoint Online, you can export your presentation as a PowerPoint file, a PDF, or even a video. To export your presentation, go to the "File" tab and select "Export." From there, you can choose the format you want to use.

Additionally, you can also share your presentation directly from PowerPoint Online by sending a link or inviting others to collaborate on the presentation with you. To share your presentation, go to the "Share" button in the top right corner and select "Invite People" or "Copy Link."

Animating Your Slides Animations can add visual interest and help keep your audience engaged during your presentation. PowerPoint Online provides several animation options, such as entrance and exit animations, emphasis animations, and movement animations. To add an animation to a slide element, simply select the element and go to the "Animations" tab. From there, you can choose the animation you want to apply, as well as set timing and triggers for the animation.

Working with Charts and Graphs Charts and graphs can help you present data and information in a clear and concise way. In PowerPoint Online, you can create a variety of charts and graphs, such as bar charts, line charts, and pie charts. To create a chart or graph, go to the "Insert" tab and select "Charts." From there, you can choose the type of chart or graph you want to create and enter your data. You can also format your chart or graph, such as changing the colors and style, adding a title, and adding labels.

Inserting Media Media, such as images, videos, and audio, can help you enhance your presentation and add visual interest. In

PowerPoint Online, you can insert media from your device, or from the web using services such as Bing Images or YouTube. To insert media, go to the "Insert" tab and select "Images" or "Media." From there, you can browse for the media you want to insert, or enter a search term if you're inserting media from the web.

Using Templates Templates are pre-designed slide layouts that you can use as a starting point for your presentation. PowerPoint Online provides a variety of templates that you can use to save time and create a professional-looking presentation. To use a template, go to the "File" tab and select "New." From there, you can browse through the available templates and select the one you want to use.

Collaborating with Others Collaborating with others can be a great way to get feedback and ideas for your presentation. In PowerPoint Online, you can share your presentation with others and work on it together in real-time. To collaborate with others, go to the "Share" button in the top right corner and select "Invite People." From there, you can enter the email addresses of the people you want to collaborate with, and set their level of access. You and your collaborators can then make changes to the presentation, add comments, and track changes in real-time.

In conclusion, PowerPoint Online is a versatile and powerful tool for creating presentations. Whether you're creating a simple slideshow or a complex presentation, PowerPoint Online provides the tools and features you need to communicate your ideas effectively. With the ability to format text and slides, insert media, work with charts and graphs, and collaborate with others, you can enhance your productivity and create engaging and professional-looking presentations using PowerPoint Online.

Chapter 8 - Introduction to OneDrive

OneDrive is Microsoft's cloud storage service that allows you to store, access, and share your files and documents from anywhere, on any device. With OneDrive, you can keep your files organized and protected, and collaborate with others in real-time. This chapter will provide an overview of OneDrive, including its features and benefits.

Features of OneDrive OneDrive offers a range of features to help you manage and access your files and documents:

- File storage: Store all of your files and documents in OneDrive, and access them from anywhere, on any device.

- File sharing: Share files and folders with others, and set permissions for who can view, edit, or download your files.

- Real-time collaboration: Work on documents together in real-time, using Office Online apps such as Word Online, Excel Online, and PowerPoint Online.

- File protection: Keep your files safe and secure with automatic backup and file versioning, and restore previous versions of your files if necessary.

- File search: Quickly search for files and documents using OneDrive's advanced search capabilities, and filter your results by file type, date, and more.

- Benefits of OneDrive OneDrive offers several benefits that can help you enhance your productivity and work more efficiently:

- Accessibility: Access your files and documents from anywhere, on any device, and work offline when necessary.

- Collaboration: Work with others in real-time, using Office Online apps, and share files and documents with others as needed.

- Organization: Keep your files organized, and easily find what you need using OneDrive's advanced search capabilities.

- Protection: Keep your files safe and secure with automatic backup and file versioning, and restore previous versions of your files if necessary.

- Integration: OneDrive integrates with Microsoft Office and other Microsoft services, making it easy to work with your files and documents.

Getting Started with OneDrive Getting started with OneDrive is easy. Simply sign in to your Microsoft account and go to the OneDrive website. From there, you can upload your files and documents, and start using OneDrive to store, access, and share your files.

Once you have set up your OneDrive account, you can start using it to store, access, and share your files and documents. There are several key features of OneDrive that you should familiarize yourself with in order to work more efficiently and effectively with OneDrive.

Uploading Files to OneDrive To upload files to OneDrive, simply go to the OneDrive website, and drag and drop your files into the OneDrive window. Alternatively, you can click the "Upload" button and select the files you want to upload. OneDrive supports a wide range of file formats, including documents, images, videos, and audio files.

Organizing Your Files in OneDrive OneDrive makes it easy to keep your files organized. You can create folders to group your files, and use tags and metadata to help you find what you're looking for. You can also sort your files by date, file type, and more, and use the search function to quickly find specific files or documents.

Sharing Files and Folders with Others OneDrive allows you to share files and folders with others, and set permissions for who can view, edit, or download your files. To share a file or folder, simply right-click on the file or folder, and select "Share." From there, you can enter the email addresses of the people you want to share the file with, and set their permissions. You can also generate a link that you can share with others, allowing them to access the file or folder without having to sign in to OneDrive.

Working with Office Online OneDrive integrates with Office Online, allowing you to work on documents, spreadsheets, and presentations from anywhere, on any device. To use Office Online, simply go to the OneDrive website, and click on the file you want to work on. The file will open in the appropriate Office Online app, and you can start working on it right away. You can also collaborate with others in real-time, using Office Online apps such as Word Online, Excel Online, and PowerPoint Online.

File Versioning and Restore OneDrive automatically backs up your files and documents, and keeps a history of all previous versions. This means that if you accidentally delete a file, or need to restore an older version of a file, you can easily do so. To access previous versions of a file, simply right-click on the file, and select "Version history." From there, you can preview and restore previous versions of the file, or download a copy of the file if necessary.

OneDrive provides a variety of tools and features to help you manage your files and folders. Whether you're working with a large number of files and folders, or simply need to keep things organized, OneDrive makes it easy to manage your files.

Renaming Files and Folders You can easily rename files and folders in OneDrive. Simply right-click on the file or folder, and select "Rename." You can then enter a new name for the file or folder. Note that renaming a file or folder will affect all other people who have access to that file or folder, so it's a good idea to make sure everyone is aware of the change.

Moving and Copying Files and Folders If you need to move or copy files and folders in OneDrive, you can simply drag and drop the files or folders to their new location. Alternatively, you can right-click on the file or folder, and select "Move to" or "Copy to." You can then select the destination folder for the file or folder. Note that moving or copying a file or folder will affect all other people who have access to that file or folder, so it's a good idea to make sure everyone is aware of the change.

Deleting Files and Folders To delete a file or folder in OneDrive, simply right-click on the file or folder, and select "Delete." Note that deleting a file or folder is permanent, and cannot be undone, so it's a good idea to be careful when deleting files and folders in OneDrive.

Managing Permissions OneDrive allows you to set permissions for who can access and edit your files and folders. To manage permissions for a file or folder, simply right-click on the file or folder, and select "Share." From there, you can add or remove people from the list of people who have access to the file or folder, and set their permissions. You can also generate a link that you can share with others, allowing them to access the file or folder without having to sign in to OneDrive.

Using OneDrive with Office Desktop Apps In addition to working with Office Online apps, you can also use OneDrive with desktop versions of Office apps, such as Word, Excel, and PowerPoint. To do this, simply save your files to OneDrive, and then open them in the desktop app. You can then work on the file as you would any other file, and the changes will be automatically saved to OneDrive. Note that if you're working with others on the same file, it's a good idea to make sure everyone is using the same version of the file, and to save your changes regularly to avoid conflicts.

OneDrive provides a variety of tools and features to help you manage your files and folders. Whether you're working with a large number of files and folders, or simply need to keep things organized, OneDrive makes it easy to manage your files. With the ability to store, access, and share your files from anywhere, on any device, OneDrive is a valuable addition to your productivity toolkit.

Chapter 9 - Sharing and Collaborating on Files with OneDrive

One of the most useful features of OneDrive is its ability to allow you to share files with others and collaborate on them in real-time. In this chapter, we will explore how to share files and folders and collaborate on them with others.

1.Sharing a file or folder

To share a file or folder in OneDrive, you need to right-click on the file or folder you want to share and select the "Share" option. You can then invite others to access the file or folder by entering their email addresses and choosing the level of access you want to grant them (view, edit, or owner).

2.Setting up permission levels

When you share a file or folder, you can choose from three permission levels: View, Edit, or Owner. View means the recipient can only view the file or folder, Edit means the recipient can make changes to the file or folder, and Owner means the recipient has full control over the file or folder.

3.Collaborating on files

OneDrive allows you to collaborate on files in real-time, meaning you can work on a document simultaneously with others. To do this, simply open the file you want to collaborate on and select the "Collaborate" option. You can then invite others to join you in the collaboration.

4.Version history

OneDrive also keeps track of all changes made to a file, so you can easily see who made changes and when. To view the version history, simply right-click on the file and select "Version history".

5.Resolving conflicts

In the event that two or more people make changes to the same part of a file at the same time, OneDrive will prompt you to resolve the conflict. To do this, simply compare the conflicting changes and choose which changes you want to keep.

6.Version history

OneDrive also keeps track of changes made to your files and folders, allowing you to see the history of revisions and even revert back to a previous version if needed. This is especially useful in cases where someone accidentally deletes or modifies something that shouldn't have been changed. To access the version history, simply right-click on the file or folder and select "Version history".

7.File recovery

In addition to version history, OneDrive also has a file recovery feature that allows you to recover deleted files for up to 30 days. This gives you peace of mind knowing that you can recover important files even if they are accidentally deleted. To recover a deleted file, go to the OneDrive recycle bin and select the file(s) you want to recover.

8.Integration with other Office 365 apps

OneDrive integrates with other Office 365 apps such as Word, Excel, and PowerPoint, allowing you to open and save files directly to OneDrive from within these apps. This makes it easier to access your files and collaborate with others, as well as ensure that your files are automatically saved and backed up.

9.File sharing options

When sharing files and folders, you have several options to choose from. For example, you can choose to give someone edit or view access, and you can also set permissions for specific individuals or groups. This allows you to have greater control over who can access your files and what they can do with them.

10.Conclusion

OneDrive is a powerful tool for sharing and collaborating on files and folders in Office 365. With features like sharing links, co-authoring, version history, and file recovery, OneDrive makes it easy to work together with others, no matter where you are or what device you're using. By leveraging these features, you can improve your productivity, streamline your workflow, and achieve more in less time.

Chapter 10 - Getting Started with Outlook Online

Introduction

Outlook Online is a web-based version of Microsoft's popular email and calendar app. It provides you with all of the functionality you need to manage your email, calendar, and contacts, all from within your web browser. In this chapter, we'll go over the basics of getting started with Outlook Online and show you how to start using it to enhance your productivity and streamline your work.

Setting up your email account

To get started with Outlook Online, you'll first need to set up your email account. This involves providing your email address and password, as well as any other information required by your email provider. Once your account is set up, you'll be able to start sending and receiving emails right away.

Navigating the user interface

Outlook Online has a simple and intuitive user interface, with all of the features you need to manage your email, calendar, and contacts located in one place. The main components of the interface include the navigation bar, the email list, the reading pane, and the calendar view. We'll take a closer look at each of these components and show you how to use them.

Sending and receiving emails

One of the core features of Outlook Online is the ability to send and receive emails. To send an email, simply click on the "New email" button, enter the recipient's email address, add a subject and message, and click "Send". To receive emails, simply click on the "Inbox" folder to view your incoming messages.

Organizing your email

Outlook Online provides a range of tools for organizing your email, such as the ability to sort messages, flag important messages, and create custom folders. You can also use the search bar to quickly find specific messages, and you can use the "Junk email" folder to manage spam and unwanted messages.

Managing your calendar

Outlook Online also provides a powerful calendar tool, allowing you to schedule appointments, set reminders, and view your schedule for the day, week, or month. You can also invite others to events and receive notifications when they accept or decline your invitations.

Managing your contacts

In addition to email and calendar, Outlook Online also provides a contacts manager that allows you to store and manage information about your contacts. You can add new contacts, edit existing contacts, and even import contacts from other email apps.

Customizing your settings

Outlook Online provides a range of customization options that allow you to personalize your email and calendar experience. For example, you can change the color scheme, add a signature, and choose which notifications you receive.

Outlook Online is a powerful web-based email client that is integrated with the Microsoft Office 365 suite. With its intuitive interface and robust features, Outlook Online makes it easy to manage your email, calendar, and contacts from anywhere with an internet connection.

Managing Your Inbox

One of the first things you'll notice about Outlook Online is its clean and simple inbox view. You can quickly sort your messages by sender, subject, or date, and use the search bar to find specific emails. You can also categorize your messages into folders, which can help you keep your inbox organized.

If you receive a lot of emails, you may want to use the "Focused Inbox" feature, which separates your important messages from the rest. You can also set up rules to automatically move certain types of emails to specific folders, such as promotional emails or newsletters.

Creating and Sending Emails

To create a new email message in Outlook Online, simply click on the "New Message" button. You can add one or more recipients to the "To" field, and include additional recipients in the "Cc" and "Bcc" fields if necessary. You can also attach files to your email, either by browsing your computer or by selecting files from OneDrive.

When you're ready to send your email, simply click the "Send" button. You can also save a draft of your email if you need to come back to it later, or schedule it to be sent at a specific time.

Managing Your Calendar

Outlook Online also includes a full-featured calendar, which makes it easy to schedule appointments, meetings, and events. You can view your calendar in either a day, week, or month view, and you can quickly create new appointments by clicking on a time slot and selecting "New Meeting."

You can also invite attendees to your meetings and events, and see their availability in real-time. This makes it easy to find a time that works for everyone, and ensures that everyone has all the necessary information for the meeting.

Managing Your Contacts

Outlook Online also includes a powerful contacts manager, which makes it easy to keep track of all your important contacts and their information. You can create new contacts, edit existing ones, and add notes to help you remember important details.

When you receive an email from a new contact, Outlook Online will automatically add them to your contacts list. You can also import contacts from other email services, such as Gmail or Yahoo! Mail, and export your contacts to other email clients or to a CSV file.

Conclusion

Outlook Online is a powerful and intuitive web-based email client that is fully integrated with the Microsoft Office 365 suite. With its clean interface, robust features, and easy-to-use calendar and contacts managers, Outlook Online makes it easy to manage your email, schedule, and contacts from anywhere with an internet connection. Whether you're a beginner or an experienced user, this chapter has provided you with a comprehensive guide to getting started with Outlook Online and making the most of its features.

Chapter 11 - Advanced Features in Outlook Online

Outlook Online is more than just an email client. It's a powerful productivity tool that offers a range of features to help you manage your communication and schedule efficiently. In this chapter, we will cover some of the advanced features that you can use in Outlook Online to enhance your productivity and work more efficiently.

1. Tasks: Outlook Online offers a built-in task management system that lets you create, edit, and keep track of tasks directly from your inbox. You can add tasks, set due dates and reminders, mark them as complete, and even categorize them using the task list.

2. Calendars: Outlook Online provides a powerful calendar that can be used to schedule appointments, events, and meetings. You can also view multiple calendars at once, including those shared with you by others, and subscribe to other users' calendars.

3. Rules: You can create email rules to automatically sort, move, or flag incoming messages based on specific criteria. For example, you can set a rule to automatically move all emails from a certain sender to a specific folder.

4. Quick Steps: Quick Steps are a series of pre-defined actions that you can use to automate repetitive tasks. For example, you can create a Quick Step to automatically flag an email and move it to a specific folder with just one click.

5. Archiving: Outlook Online offers an archiving feature that allows you to store old or less important emails in an archive folder. This helps to keep your inbox organized and reduces clutter.

6. Focused Inbox: The Focused Inbox feature in Outlook Online separates your most important emails from the rest, allowing you to focus on the messages that matter most. You can also train the feature to better understand your email habits and what you consider to be important.

7. Search: Outlook Online provides a powerful search tool that can help you quickly find the information you need. You can search for specific emails, appointments, or contacts, and even use advanced search operators to find exactly what you're looking for.

8. Skype for Business: Outlook Online integrates with Skype for Business, which allows you to initiate voice or video calls, send instant messages, or schedule online meetings directly from your inbox.

In conclusion, the advanced features in Outlook Online can help you streamline your workflow and improve your productivity. Whether you're managing tasks, scheduling appointments, or organizing your inbox, the advanced features in Outlook Online are designed to help you work more efficiently and effectively.

Chapter 12 - Using Teams for Communication and Collaboration

Microsoft Teams is a communication and collaboration platform that allows teams to work together effectively in a virtual environment. In this chapter, we will explore the key features of Teams and how you can use it to enhance your productivity.

1. Channels: Teams allows you to organize your communication and collaboration by creating different channels for different projects or teams. For example, you can create a channel for a specific project and invite relevant team members to join.

2. Chat: The chat feature in Teams allows you to have real-time conversations with your team members. You can also share files, images, and videos in chat, making it a convenient way to collaborate and exchange information.

3. Meetings: Teams provides video and audio conferencing capabilities, allowing you to have virtual meetings with your team members. You can schedule meetings in advance, share your screen, and record meetings for future reference.

4. Collaboration Tools: Teams integrates with other Microsoft 365 applications, such as Word, Excel, and

PowerPoint, making it easy for teams to collaborate on documents in real-time. You can also use the built-in version control feature to keep track of changes made to documents.

5. Integrations: Teams integrates with a wide range of third-party applications, including Trello, Asana, and Github, making it easy to integrate your existing workflows and tools into Teams.

6. File Storage: Teams includes OneDrive, a cloud-based file storage solution, allowing teams to store, access, and share files from anywhere. Teams also includes robust security and compliance features, making it easy to meet your organization's data security and regulatory requirements.

7. Mobile Accessibility: Teams also has mobile apps available for both iOS and Android devices, allowing you to access your Teams account and collaborate with your team from anywhere, at any time. The mobile app provides a seamless user experience, allowing you to access all of the features of the desktop app on your mobile device.

8. Notifications: Teams provides real-time notifications to keep you informed of important updates, messages, and meeting invitations. You can customize your notification settings to ensure that you receive the notifications that are most important to you.

9. Tasks and To-Do Lists: Teams includes a built-in task management system, allowing you to create and assign tasks to team members, set deadlines, and track progress.

This feature makes it easy for teams to stay organized and on track, even in a virtual environment.

10. Third-Party Integrations: Teams integrates with a wide range of third-party tools and services, such as Salesforce, Slack, and Jira, allowing you to bring all of your tools and workflows together in one place. This integration makes it easy to manage your work and collaborate with your team, no matter what tools and services you are using.

11. Compliance and Security: Teams is designed to meet the highest standards of compliance and security, making it a secure and reliable platform for collaboration and communication. Teams uses encryption and other security measures to protect your data and ensure that your communication and collaboration are always secure.

12. Meetings and Video Conferencing: Teams makes it easy to host virtual meetings and video conferences, whether you are connecting with coworkers, clients, or customers. You can schedule and join meetings directly from Teams, and use features such as screen sharing, file sharing, and video conferencing to collaborate and communicate in real-time.

13. Recording Meetings: Teams also allows you to record your meetings and video conferences, making it easy to review and share important information with your team or other stakeholders. The recorded files can be stored and accessed in the cloud, so you always have access to the most up-to-date information.

14. Chat and Instant Messaging: Teams provides a built-in chat and instant messaging platform, allowing you to

exchange messages with your team and colleagues in real-time. Whether you are discussing a project, answering a question, or simply chatting with coworkers, Teams makes it easy to stay connected and engaged with your team.

15. File Management and Sharing: Teams includes a comprehensive file management and sharing system, allowing you to upload, store, and share files with your team. You can access your files from anywhere, at any time, and collaborate with your team in real-time, making it easy to keep your projects on track and moving forward.

16. Customization and Branding: Teams provides a range of customization and branding options, allowing you to personalize your Teams account and align it with your company's brand and identity. Whether you want to add custom backgrounds, logos, or custom themes, Teams makes it easy to customize your experience and make Teams your own.

In conclusion, Teams is a powerful and feature-rich platform that provides everything you need to communicate, collaborate, and get work done. With its user-friendly interface, real-time collaboration tools, and mobile accessibility, Teams makes it easy to work with your team, no matter where you are or what you are working on. Whether you are a beginner or an experienced user, Teams is the complete collaboration platform for enhancing your productivity in 2023.

Chapter 13 - Managing Your Tasks and To-Do List with Planner

Microsoft Planner is a feature within Office 365 that allows you to manage your tasks and to-do lists in an organized and efficient way. It is designed to help teams stay on track and complete their tasks on time. In this chapter, we will explore how to get started with Planner and how to use it to manage your tasks and to-do lists.

Getting Started with Planner

To start using Planner, you will need to have an Office 365 subscription. Once you have an account, you can access Planner from the Office 365 app launcher. To do this, click on the app launcher icon (the nine dots in the upper left corner of your screen), and then select Planner from the list of available apps.

Creating a Plan

The first step in using Planner is to create a plan. To do this, click on the "Create Plan" button on the Planner home screen. Then, give your plan a name, choose the team you want to work with, and select a group to assign tasks to.

Adding Tasks

Once you have created a plan, you can start adding tasks. To do this, simply click on the "Add Task" button on the plan's page. Then, enter a task name, add a due date, and assign the task to a team member.

Organizing Tasks with Buckets

Planner allows you to organize your tasks into buckets. Buckets are essentially categories that help you categorize and prioritize your tasks. To create a bucket, simply click on the "Add Bucket" button on the plan's page, give the bucket a name, and then add tasks to it.

Tracking Progress

One of the key benefits of using Planner is that it makes it easy to track your progress. You can see the status of your tasks, who is responsible for each task, and when tasks are due. You can also add comments to tasks and attach files to them. This makes it easy to keep everyone on the same page and to communicate effectively.

Microsoft Planner is a valuable tool for managing your tasks and to-do lists. With its user-friendly interface and powerful features, it can help you stay on track and complete your tasks on time. Whether you're working alone or with a team, Planner is an essential tool for anyone who wants to enhance their productivity in 2023.

Chapter 14 - Setting Up and Using OneNote for Notes and Note-Taking

OneNote is a powerful digital note-taking tool that comes with Office 365. It allows you to organize all of your notes, thoughts, and ideas in one place, making it an ideal tool for students, professionals, and anyone who wants to be more productive. In this chapter, we'll show you how to set up and use OneNote to take notes, store information, and keep track of your tasks and ideas.

Getting Started with OneNote

To get started with OneNote, you'll first need to sign in to your Office 365 account. Once you've signed in, you can access OneNote by clicking on the OneNote app in the Office 365 app launcher.

When you first open OneNote, you'll see a blank notebook with no pages. To create a new page, simply click on the "New Page" button at the top of the screen. You can also create a new section by clicking on the "New Section" button.

Taking Notes with OneNote

OneNote is designed to make taking notes easy and intuitive. To start taking notes, simply click anywhere on the page and start typing. You can format your text by using the toolbar at the top of the screen. You can also add images, tables, and other media to your notes by using the "Insert" menu.

Organizing Your Notes

OneNote allows you to organize your notes into sections and pages, making it easy to find what you need when you need it. You can create new sections and pages by using the "New Section" and "New Page" buttons. You can also move pages and sections around by clicking and dragging them.

Using OneNote for Tasks and To-Do Lists

OneNote is also a great tool for keeping track of your tasks and to-do lists. To create a to-do list, simply create a new page and start typing. You can use the "Check Box" option in the toolbar to create checkboxes for each task. When you've completed a task, simply check the box.

Sharing and Collaborating with OneNote

One of the great things about OneNote is that it allows you to share your notes and collaborate with others. To share a notebook, simply right-click on the notebook and select "Share". You can then enter the email addresses of the people you want to share the notebook with. You can also set permissions to allow others to edit or view the notebook.

OneNote is a powerful and versatile tool that can help you take better notes, stay organized, and get more done. Whether you're a student, professional, or anyone who wants to be more productive, OneNote is an excellent tool that can help you achieve your goals. In this chapter, we've shown you how to set up and use OneNote to take notes, store information, and keep track of your tasks and ideas.

Chapter 15 - Exploring Additional Office 365 Apps and Services

In addition to the core apps covered in this guide, Microsoft Office 365 also includes several other applications and services that can help you be more productive and efficient in your work. In this chapter, we'll introduce you to a few of these additional tools.

1. OneNote Class Notebook: OneNote Class Notebook is a powerful tool for teachers that allows them to create a shared notebook for their class, including students, teachers, and other instructors. It's a great way to keep everyone organized and on track, and it's easy to set up and use.Getting started with OneNote Class Notebook is easy. Simply create a notebook for your class, and invite your students to join. From there, you can organize your content into separate sections for each subject or topic, and use OneNote's rich formatting and multimedia capabilities to create engaging and interactive lesson materials.OneNote Class Notebook also provides teachers with a variety of tools to help manage their classroom. For example, you can set up a student-only section within the notebook, where students can collaborate and share ideas without fear of losing or overwriting each other's work.Additionally, you can use the "Collaborate" tab in

OneNote to send announcements, messages, or questions to your students. You can also use OneNote's "Tag" feature to quickly and easily flag items for follow-up, such as assignments that need grading or feedback.In conclusion, OneNote Class Notebook is a powerful and versatile tool that can help teachers and students alike to be more organized and productive in the classroom. Whether you are looking to create engaging and interactive lesson materials, keep track of student progress, or simply streamline your classwork, OneNote Class Notebook has something to offer. So why not give it a try today and see how it can enhance your productivity in the classroom!

2. StaffHub: StaffHub is a scheduling and shift management tool designed specifically for hourly workers and front-line staff. It helps managers create schedules, communicate with staff, and track time off requests, all from within the Office 365 platform. Microsoft StaffHub is a cloud-based platform that makes it easy for managers and staff to organize work schedules, communicate and collaborate with team members, and access important information and tools. With StaffHub, you can easily manage your employees' schedules, communicate with them, and ensure that everyone is on the same page. This chapter will guide you through the basics of getting started with StaffHub.

Setting Up Your StaffHub Account To get started with StaffHub, you'll first need to set up your account. You can do this by visiting the StaffHub website, or by downloading the StaffHub app from the Microsoft Store.

To create an account, simply enter your email address and password, and follow the on-screen instructions.

Understanding the User Interface Once you've set up your account, you'll be taken to the StaffHub user interface. The interface is designed to be intuitive and user-friendly, making it easy for you to navigate and find the information you need. You'll see a list of your team members, as well as a calendar view that displays your schedule and your team's schedule. You can also access important information and tools, such as shift requests and availability, by clicking on the appropriate tab.

Managing Your Team's Schedules One of the main features of StaffHub is the ability to manage your team's schedules. You can add shifts, assign employees to specific shifts, and approve or decline shift requests. You can also view your team's availability and schedule in real-time, making it easy to make any necessary changes.

Communicating with Team Members StaffHub also makes it easy for you to communicate with your team members. You can send messages directly to individual team members, or to the entire team. You can also use StaffHub to create announcements that will be visible to all team members.

Accessing Important Information and Tools In addition to managing schedules and communicating with team members, StaffHub also provides access to important information and tools. You can view shift reports, employee information, and other important data. You can also use StaffHub to access other Microsoft Office apps, such as Word and Excel, making it easy to get the information you need, when you need it.

Customizing Your StaffHub Experience Finally, StaffHub gives you the ability to customize your experience to fit your needs. You can adjust your notification settings, change your password, and access a range of other settings to help you get the most out of StaffHub.

In conclusion, StaffHub is a powerful tool for managers and staff who want to stay organized, communicate effectively, and access important information and tools. Whether you're managing a small team or a large organization, StaffHub can help you improve your productivity and streamline your workflow.

3. Forms: Forms is a powerful survey and data collection tool that you can use to collect data from customers, employees, or anyone else. With Forms, you can create professional-looking surveys, quizzes, and questionnaires, and then easily share them with others.

Getting started with Forms

To get started with Forms, you'll need to access it through the Office 365 app launcher. To do this, simply click on the waffle icon in the upper left-hand corner of your screen and select Forms from the list of available apps. Once you're in the Forms app, you'll be able to create new forms, edit existing ones, and view responses.

Creating a new form

To create a new form, simply click on the "New form" button in the upper right-hand corner of your screen. You'll then be prompted to choose a template for your form, or you can start from scratch by clicking "Blank form". From there, you'll be able to add questions, sections, and other elements to your form to create the survey or quiz that you need.

Adding questions to your form

One of the key elements of any form is the questions that you ask. Forms provides a variety of question types that you can use to gather information, including multiple choice questions, rating scales, and open-ended text questions. To add a question to your form, simply click on the "Add question" button and select the type of question that you want to add. Then, type in your question and add any additional options that you need.

Formatting and customizing your form

Forms also allows you to format and customize your form to meet your specific needs. You can change the color scheme, font style, and background image for your form, and you can even add images, videos, and other multimedia elements to make your form more engaging for your audience.

Sharing and distributing your form

Once your form is complete, you'll need to share it with the people who you want to take it. Forms provides a variety of options for sharing your form, including emailing it to specific individuals, embedding it on your website or blog, or sharing it on social media. You can also set permissions for who can view, edit, or respond to your form, so you can control who has access to the information that you collect.

Collecting and analyzing responses

Once you start receiving responses to your form, you can use the Forms app to view and analyze the results. You'll be able to see a summary of the responses for each question, as well as individual responses, so you can gain insights into the information that you've collected. You can also export your data to Excel or another program for further analysis if needed.

In conclusion, Forms is a powerful and versatile tool within Microsoft Office 365 that can help you gather information and insights quickly and easily. Whether you're creating a survey, quiz, or simply gathering data, Forms provides a simple and efficient solution that can help you get the information you need.

4. PowerApps: PowerApps is a low-code app platform that allows you to build custom apps to meet your specific needs. You can use PowerApps to automate business

processes, create custom forms, and more, without needing any coding skills.

5. Stream: Stream is a video platform that makes it easy to share and discover videos within your organization. With Stream, you can upload and share videos, embed videos on your team sites, and discover videos that others have shared.

These are just a few of the additional apps and services included in Office 365. Whether you're looking for a tool to help you manage your time, communicate with your team, or automate your business processes, Office 365 has you covered.

Another app included in Office 365 is Sway. Sway is a digital storytelling app that allows you to create engaging and interactive presentations, reports, and newsletters. Sway is ideal for creating engaging and interactive presentations, reports, and newsletters.

Office 365 also includes a video conferencing app called Skype for Business. Skype for Business allows you to conduct virtual meetings and video conferencing with colleagues and clients from anywhere in the world. You can use Skype for Business to share your screen, send instant messages, and make voice and video calls.

In addition to these apps, Office 365 also includes a suite of security and compliance tools such as Exchange Online Protection, Advanced Threat Protection, and Compliance Manager. These tools help you protect your organization's sensitive information, keep your data safe, and comply with industry regulations.

Finally, Office 365 also includes a cloud-based phone system called Phone System. Phone System allows you to manage calls and voicemail in the cloud, and to use your existing phone numbers with your Office 365 account. With Phone System, you can take advantage of advanced features such as call forwarding, voicemail-to-text, and call delegation.

In conclusion, Office 365 offers a suite of powerful apps and services to enhance your productivity. From forms, sway, and Skype for Business to security and compliance tools, Phone System, and more, there's an app or service for just about every need. As you continue to work with Office 365, be sure to explore these additional apps and services to see how they can help you work more efficiently and effectively.

Chapter 16 - Customizing Your Office 365 Experience

One of the best things about Microsoft Office 365 is its versatility and ability to be customized to fit your individual needs. In this chapter, you will learn how to make the most of Office 365 by customizing your experience to suit your unique requirements.

Customizing the Office 365 User Interface

The Office 365 user interface can be customized to make it more user-friendly and to streamline your workflow. You can do this by modifying the look and feel of the interface, adjusting settings, and rearranging the layout.

To customize the Office 365 interface, go to the settings section by clicking on your profile picture or initials in the top right corner. From there, you can select "View all Office settings" and then "General." From this menu, you can adjust the look and feel of Office 365, including the background color and font size.

You can also rearrange the layout of the interface to make it more efficient. For example, you can move frequently used tools and apps to the top of the screen for easy access.

Customizing Office 365 Apps

Each of the apps within Office 365 can be customized as well. For example, in Word Online, you can adjust settings such as margins, page orientation, and font size. In Excel Online, you can customize the number of worksheets, the gridlines, and the calculation options. In PowerPoint Online, you can adjust the slide size, orientation, and background.

Additionally, you can add custom templates, themes, and styles to each of the Office 365 apps. This can make it easier to create consistent, professional-looking documents, spreadsheets, and presentations.

Customizing Your Office 365 Account

Finally, you can customize your Office 365 account itself by adjusting settings such as privacy, language, and time zone. To access these settings, click on your profile picture or initials in the top right corner and select "Account." From here, you can make changes to your account settings and manage your billing information.

In conclusion, customizing your Office 365 experience can help you make the most of the platform and streamline your workflow. Whether you're a beginner or an experienced user, taking the time to personalize your Office 365 experience is well worth the effort.

Chapter 17 - Troubleshooting Common Office 365 Issues

Office 365 is a robust suite of productivity tools, but like any software, it can experience issues from time to time. The good news is that many common issues can be easily resolved with a few troubleshooting steps. In this chapter, we'll cover some of the most common problems you may encounter and how to resolve them.

1. Login Issues: If you're having trouble logging into your Office 365 account, make sure you're using the correct email address and password. If you've forgotten your password, you can reset it by clicking the "Forgot password" link on the login page. If you're still having trouble, check that your account hasn't been blocked or suspended due to suspicious activity.

2. Slow Performance: If you're experiencing slow performance when using Office 365, it may be due to a slow internet connection. Make sure your internet speed meets the minimum requirements for Office 365. If your connection is fast enough, try clearing your browser cache and cookies, or switch to a different browser.

3. File Not Saving: If you're working on a document and it won't save, it may be due to a lack of storage space in your OneDrive account. To resolve this issue, you can either purchase more storage or move some of your files to a different location.

4. Cannot Find a File: If you're having trouble finding a file, make sure you're searching in the correct location. If you're still having trouble, try using the advanced search options to narrow your results.

5. Issues with Sharing and Collaborating: If you're having trouble sharing or collaborating on a file, make sure the person you're sharing with has the necessary permissions to access the file. You can also check the sharing settings on the file to see if there are any restrictions in place.

6. Error Messages: If you're receiving an error message, it may be due to a temporary issue with the Office 365 servers. Try again later, and if the issue persists, contact Microsoft support for assistance.

These are just a few of the most common issues you may encounter while using Office 365. By following these troubleshooting steps, you should be able to resolve most problems quickly and easily. If you're still having trouble, don't hesitate to reach out to Microsoft support for additional assistance.

Chapter 18 - Making the Most of Office 365 Mobile Apps

In today's fast-paced world, mobile devices have become an integral part of our daily lives. Whether you're at home, at work, or on the go, you need access to your files, emails, and other important information at all times. That's where the Office 365 mobile apps come in. These apps are designed to help you be productive no matter where you are, giving you the ability to work with your Office 365 documents and data on your mobile device.

This chapter will provide you with an overview of the Office 365 mobile apps and show you how to use them to their full potential.

1. Overview of Office 365 Mobile Apps

The Office 365 mobile apps include Word, Excel, PowerPoint, OneDrive, Outlook, Teams, and more. These apps are available for iOS and Android devices, and can be downloaded from the App Store or Google Play Store. With the Office 365 mobile apps, you can work with your Office 365 documents, spreadsheets, presentations, and other files from anywhere, at any time.

2. Getting Started with Office 365 Mobile Apps

To get started with the Office 365 mobile apps, you'll need to download the apps from the App Store or Google Play Store. Once you've downloaded the apps, you'll need to sign in with your Office 365 account. You'll then be able to access your files, emails, and other information stored in your Office 365 account.

3. Using Word, Excel, and PowerPoint on Mobile Devices

The Word, Excel, and PowerPoint mobile apps allow you to create, edit, and view your Office 365 documents, spreadsheets, and presentations on the go. You'll have access to all the same features and functionality that you have on your desktop, so you can work on your files no matter where you are.

4. Using OneDrive on Mobile Devices

OneDrive is an online storage service that allows you to store and access your files from anywhere, at any time. With the OneDrive mobile app, you can easily access your files and folders, as well as upload and download files to and from your OneDrive account.

5. Using Outlook on Mobile Devices

The Outlook mobile app provides a convenient way to access your email, calendar, and contacts while on the go. You can send and receive emails, schedule appointments, and manage your contacts just as you would on your desktop.

6. Using Teams on Mobile Devices

Teams is a collaboration platform that allows you to communicate and work together with your team, no matter where you are. With the Teams mobile app, you can participate in conversations, join meetings, and access all the same features and functionality that you have on your desktop.

7. Making the Most of Office 365 Mobile Apps

With the Office 365 mobile apps, you have the ability to be productive no matter where you are. Whether you're working on a document, editing a spreadsheet, or participating in a meeting, the Office 365 mobile apps make it easy for you to work with your Office 365 files and information from your mobile device. So be sure to take advantage of these apps to maximize your productivity and get the most out of your Office 365 experience.

Chapter 19 - Tips and Tricks for Enhanced Productivity in Office 365

Office 365 is a powerful platform that offers a vast range of features and tools to enhance your productivity. Whether you are a beginner or an experienced user, there are always ways to optimize your use of the platform to get the most out of it. In this chapter, we'll discuss some tips and tricks that will help you work more efficiently and effectively in Office 365.

1. Keyboard shortcuts: Keyboard shortcuts are a quick and easy way to navigate and perform tasks in Office 365. For example, you can use the keyboard shortcut Ctrl + N to create a new document in Word Online. There are many other keyboard shortcuts available in Office 365, and you can find a comprehensive list by searching online or within the app's help menu.

2. Use templates: Office 365 provides a wide range of templates that you can use to create professional-looking documents, presentations, and spreadsheets quickly and easily. You can find templates for resumes, flyers, invoices, and more. Using a template will save you time and effort compared to creating a document from scratch.

3. Collaborate in real-time: With Office 365, you can work on documents, presentations, and spreadsheets with others

in real-time. This means you can see changes made by others as they happen and provide feedback in the moment. This feature can be especially useful for group projects and presentations.

4. Integrate with other apps: Office 365 integrates with a range of other apps and services, such as OneDrive, Teams, and SharePoint. This integration makes it easy to access your files and collaborate with others, no matter where you are.

5. Use OneDrive for document management: OneDrive is a cloud-based storage service that is integrated with Office 365. You can use it to store, access, and share your files and documents from anywhere. With OneDrive, you can also collaborate on documents with others in real-time.

6. Automate tasks with Microsoft Power Automate: Microsoft Power Automate is a tool that allows you to automate repetitive tasks in Office 365. For example, you can use it to automatically send emails or notifications when a specific event occurs, such as when a new file is added to OneDrive.

7. Make use of the Office 365 mobile app: The Office 365 mobile app allows you to access and work on your documents, presentations, and spreadsheets from anywhere, on any device. The app is available for both iOS and Android devices and is a great way to stay productive on the go.

8. Quick Access Toolbar: The Quick Access Toolbar is a customizable toolbar that you can use to access frequently used commands in Office 365 apps. You can

add commands to the toolbar by right-clicking on them and selecting Add to Quick Access Toolbar.

9. File Sharing: Office 365 allows you to share files with other people easily. When you share a file, you can choose to give others editing or viewing access. You can also set up a password for the file or add an expiration date for the link.

10. Schedule Emails: If you need to send an email at a later time, you can schedule the email in Outlook. To schedule an email, you will need to go to the File menu and select the Delay Delivery option.

11. Using Themes: Themes are a great way to add some personality to your Office 365 documents. You can access the themes by going to the Design tab in Word, Excel, or PowerPoint.

12. Co-Authoring: Co-authoring is a feature that allows you to work on the same document with multiple people at the same time. This feature is available in Word, PowerPoint, and OneNote.

By following these tips and tricks, you can take your productivity in Office 365 to the next level. Remember to always keep exploring the features and capabilities of Office 365, as new updates and features are released regularly.

Chapter 20 - Taking Your Office 365 Skills to the Next Level.

It is important to continue learning and growing your knowledge. Here are some tips for doing so:

1. Explore additional Office 365 apps and services: Office 365 offers a wide range of apps and services beyond the core productivity tools covered in this guide. Consider exploring and learning about other apps such as Stream, Power Apps, and Power Automate to expand your productivity toolkit.

2. Join the Office 365 Community: The Office 365 Community is a great place to connect with other Office 365 users, ask questions, and learn new tips and tricks. Join forums and discussion boards, or attend local Office 365 user groups to connect with others in your community.

3. Utilize online resources: There are numerous online resources available to help you continue learning and growing your Office 365 skills. Consider taking online courses or watching tutorials on websites like LinkedIn Learning or YouTube.

4. Take advantage of new features and updates: Office 365 is continually updating with new features and functionality. Stay up-to-date by regularly checking the Office 365 Roadmap or following the Office 365 blog to learn about new features and updates.

5. Practice makes perfect: The best way to continue growing your Office 365 skills is to use the platform regularly. Consider finding new ways to integrate Office 365 into your daily workflow, and look for opportunities to apply the tools and techniques you have learned. Keep practicing and learning: The best way to get better with Office 365 is to continue using it regularly. As you work on new projects, try out different features and tools to become more proficient. You can also attend online courses, watch tutorials or read blogs to learn about new features and updates.

6. Take advantage of online resources: Microsoft provides a wide range of online resources and support for Office 365 users. From the Office 365 community to the Microsoft support center, there are many resources available that can help you improve your skills and get answers to your questions.

7. Attend webinars and workshops: Microsoft also offers webinars and workshops on different topics related to Office 365. These can be a great way to learn about new features, get hands-on training, and interact with other Office 365 users.

8. Utilize keyboard shortcuts: Keyboard shortcuts can be a quick and efficient way to get things done in Office 365. Take some time to learn the most commonly used

shortcuts for the apps you use the most to boost your productivity.

9. Customize your Office 365 experience: You can customize your Office 365 experience by setting up personal preferences, creating custom templates, and organizing your apps and services in a way that works best for you.

By taking these steps, you can continue to improve your Office 365 skills and become even more productive. Whether you are a beginner or an experienced user, there is always something new to learn and explore in Office 365.

By following these tips and continuing to learn and grow your Office 365 skills, you will be able to maximize your productivity and take your use of Office 365 to the next level. Whether you are just getting started or have been using Office 365 for years, there is always something new to learn and discover.

Chapter 21 - Managing and Securing Your Data with Office 365 Security Features

One of the most important aspects of using Office 365 is ensuring the security and privacy of your data. With the rise of cyber attacks and data breaches, it's essential to understand the security features provided by Office 365 and how to use them to protect your information. This chapter will introduce you to the various security features available in Office 365 and provide you with tips on how to use them to secure your data.

1. Multi-Factor Authentication (MFA)

Multi-Factor Authentication is a security feature that adds an extra layer of protection to your Office 365 account by requiring you to provide two or more forms of authentication. This means that in addition to your password, you will be prompted to provide another form of authentication such as a security code sent to your phone, a fingerprint or a smart card. This feature helps to ensure that only authorized users have access to your Office 365 account and reduces the risk of unauthorized access.

2. Data Loss Prevention (DLP)

Data Loss Prevention is a feature that helps to protect sensitive information in Office 365 by identifying and preventing the accidental or intentional sharing of sensitive data. DLP uses policies to identify sensitive information and prevents it from being shared outside of your organization or with unauthorized users. For example, if you attempt to send an email containing sensitive information, Office 365 will prompt you with a warning and give you the option to either send the email or cancel the action.

3. Encryption

Office 365 uses encryption to secure your data both in transit and at rest. Data in transit is encrypted while it is being transmitted over the internet, while data at rest is encrypted when it is stored on Office 365 servers. This helps to prevent unauthorized access to your data and ensures that your information is protected even if it falls into the hands of an attacker.

4. Auditing and Reporting

Office 365 provides auditing and reporting capabilities that allow you to monitor user activity and track changes to your data. This includes logging of user activity, changes made to files, and access to sensitive information. This information can be used to detect and prevent security incidents, as well as to comply with regulatory requirements.

5. Compliance

Office 365 provides a variety of tools and features to help you comply with various regulatory requirements and industry standards. This includes features such as data retention and eDiscovery, which allow you to preserve and recover data as needed for legal purposes.

6. Security Best Practices

In addition to the security features provided by Office 365, it's important to follow security best practices to keep your data secure. This includes using strong and unique passwords, regularly updating your security settings, and being aware of phishing scams and other security threats.

In conclusion, Office 365 provides a wide range of security features to help you protect your data and enhance your overall security posture. By using these features and following best practices, you can ensure that your data is secure and protected while you enjoy the benefits of using Office 365.

Chapter 22 - Integrating Office 365 with Other Applications and Services

Office 365 is designed to be flexible and compatible with a wide range of other applications and services, which means that you can easily integrate it into your existing workflows and systems. This can help to increase your productivity, streamline your work processes, and ensure that your data is always accessible, even when you're working on the go.

One of the most popular integrations is with Microsoft Power Automate (formerly known as Microsoft Flow). Power Automate allows you to automate repetitive tasks, such as sending emails, copying files from one location to another, or creating events in your calendar. This can save you a lot of time and effort, and ensure that your work is completed accurately and efficiently.

Another popular integration is with Microsoft Power Apps, which is a platform for creating custom business apps. With Power Apps, you can create custom applications that integrate with your Office 365 data and automate your work processes. This can help you to improve your productivity and better manage your data.

In addition to these Microsoft tools, there are many other services and applications that can be integrated with Office 365, including:

- SharePoint: SharePoint is a platform for creating and managing websites, and it can be integrated with Office 365 to provide a centralized location for your files and documents.

- OneDrive for Business: OneDrive for Business is a cloud-based storage service that can be integrated with Office 365, allowing you to store and access your files and documents from anywhere.

- Microsoft Teams: Microsoft Teams is a collaboration platform that can be integrated with Office 365 to provide a central location for team communication, file sharing, and collaboration.

- Skype for Business: Skype for Business is a communication tool that can be integrated with Office 365 to provide voice and video calls, instant messaging, and screen sharing.

- Yammer: Yammer is a social network for businesses that can be integrated with Office 365 to provide a centralized location for communication and collaboration within your organization.

Integrating Office 365 with other applications and services can be a great way to enhance your productivity and streamline your work processes. Whether you're using Microsoft tools or other third-party services, there are many options available to help you get the most out of Office 365.

Chapter 23 - Maximizing the Benefits of Office 365 for Teams and Organizations.

Office 365 provides a range of tools and services that enable teams and organizations to work more efficiently and effectively. To maximize the benefits of Office 365, it is important to understand the features and capabilities that are available and to put them to use in the right way.

One of the key benefits of Office 365 is increased collaboration and teamwork. Teams can work together on projects and documents in real-time, using tools such as SharePoint, OneDrive, and Teams. This helps to increase productivity and reduce the time it takes to complete tasks, as team members can share information, resources, and insights more easily.

Another benefit of Office 365 is improved communication. With tools such as Outlook, Teams, and Yammer, organizations can communicate more effectively and efficiently. Teams can stay in touch, share information, and work together, even when they are in different locations.

Office 365 also provides a range of security features to help protect sensitive data and keep it safe. This includes data encryption, data loss prevention, and multi-factor authentication, among others. These features help organizations to meet their data protection and privacy obligations, as well as to keep their data secure and confidential.

In addition to these benefits, Office 365 also offers a range of tools and services for streamlining business processes. For example, organizations can use PowerApps to create custom business applications that automate workflows and streamline processes. They can also use Power BI to gain insights into business data and make informed decisions.

To maximize the benefits of Office 365 for teams and organizations, it is important to make the most of the tools and services that are available. This means taking the time to understand what each tool does, how it works, and how it can be used to support business objectives. It also means being proactive in using Office 365 to improve teamwork, communication, and productivity.

Organizations can also maximize the benefits of Office 365 by integrating it with other systems and services. For example, they can use Office 365 with CRM systems, such as Salesforce, to manage customer interactions and relationships more effectively. They can also integrate Office 365 with project management tools, such as Trello, to help teams to manage tasks, deadlines, and milestones.

In conclusion, Office 365 provides a range of tools and services that can help teams and organizations to work more efficiently and effectively. To maximize the benefits of Office 365, it is important to understand the features and capabilities that are available, to use them in the right way, and to integrate Office 365 with other systems and services as needed. By doing so, organizations can improve teamwork, communication, security, and productivity, and help to support their business objectives.

Thank you for choosing this book as a guide to exploring the vast capabilities of Office 365. We hope that you have found the information in these pages to be helpful, informative, and useful in enhancing your productivity and improving your workflow.

The authors and publishers have worked hard to provide you with a comprehensive and up-to-date resource for Office 365, and we would like to extend our sincerest gratitude for your support.

We would like to thank you for taking the time to read through this book and hope that it has been a valuable resource for you. If you have any suggestions or feedback, please don't hesitate to reach out to us.

We wish you the best of luck in your continued exploration of Office 365 and look forward to the opportunity to continue serving your learning needs.

Thank you again for choosing this book and for your support.

We hope you enjoyed reading this book on Office 365 and found it helpful in improving your productivity and efficiency with the suite of apps and services. As a valued reader, we would be incredibly grateful if you could take a few minutes to leave a review of the book on Amazon..

Your feedback and opinions matter to us, as they help us understand what works well and what could be improved in our future books. Your review also helps other readers discover this book and make informed decisions about whether it's the right fit for them.

Thank you in advance for your time and support. We look forward to hearing from you soon!